Will it pop?

Written by Jane Langford

Collins

Things pop up ...

and things go pop!

This T-Rex pops up.

a pop up ship

Will jack in the box pop up?

Yes!

This will fizz ...

then pop!

She puffs!

Will it pop?

Will a pin pop this?

Yes!

/th/

1
2
3
4
5

14

 Review: After reading

Use your assessment from hearing the children read to choose any GPCs, words or tricky words that need additional practice.

Read 1: Decoding

- Read page 2 and ask: What does **pop up** mean? (e.g. *go up, jump towards the ceiling*) Focus on page 3 and ask: What does **pop** mean here? (e.g. *go bang, burst*)
- Point to **things** on page 2, asking the children to sound and blend out loud. Repeat for **this** on page 8. Then turn to page 9 and encourage the children to blend in their heads, silently, before reading the words aloud.
- Look at the "I spy sounds" pages (14–15) together. Point to the puppet theatre and say "theatre", emphasising the /th/ sound. Ask the children to find other things that start with the /th/ sound. (e.g. *thistles, thatch, thermometer, three*). Repeat for words that start with /sh/. (e.g. *shell, sharpener, sheep, shark, shapes, shoe, ship*)

Read 2: Prosody

- Focus on words that sound like the action they are describing (onomatopoeia).
- On page 8, encourage the children to read **fizz**, emphasising the /z/ sound. On page 9, point to **pop**. Ask: Can you read this so that it sounds like a bubble bursting?
- Encourage the children to read both pages aloud, emphasising the onomatopoeic words.
- Did the children pause at the ellipsis? If necessary, point out the ellipsis and explain that we need to pause here (to wait and see what happens next). Ask the children to reread pages 8 and 9, pausing and with emphasis.

Read 3: Comprehension

- Ask the children if they have seen, or played with, things that popped up, or popped. Encourage the children to describe them and explain their favourites.
- Ask the children:
  - On page 6: Why might you get a surprise when you open this box? (e.g. *because the doll – Jack – suddenly pops up*)
  - On page 11: Do you think it will pop? Why? (e.g. *yes, because bubbles always burst*)
- Encourage the children to think of other things that pop up or might pop (burst). (e.g. *a puppet pops up in a play; tyres, balls, popcorn can pop*)